Mer
Happy Hanukkah!

Celebrate God's Love

Hanukkah and Christmas Fact and Fiction

Joan Lipis

Love
Poppi & Grandma
Frazzano

CELEBRATE GOD'S LOVE

Produced by Palm Tree Publications
A Division of Palm Tree Productions
Keller, Texas, U.S.A.
Printed in The U.S.A.

www.palmtreeproductions.net

Cover Design & Interior Layout: Wendy K. Walters

To contact the author:

web | www.novea.org
email | novea@novea.org

Novea Ministries
P.O. Box 62592
Colorado Springs, CO
USA 80962

Contents

1 Introduction
God is Love

3 Chapter One
Hanukkah

5 Chapter Two
The Hanukkah Christmas Connection

21 Chapter Three
The Beginning of the Gospel about Yeshua

29 Chapter Four
The Incarnation

33 Chapter Five
Jesus and Hanukkah

47 Appendix
PARTIAL LIST OF PROPHECIES CONCERNING YESHUA

Introduction

God is Love

During the winter month of December, many people around the world celebrate two very different holidays—different, yet similar.

They are different because they are celebrated by different people. The Jewish people celebrate Hanukkah, while the Gentiles (both Christian and non-Christian) celebrate Christmas.

These two holidays are similar in that they both celebrate God's love. They are similar also in another very important aspect—they are both man-made. God gave the Jewish people very specific holy days to observe, but neither Hanukkah nor Christmas is one of them.

The holidays are similar in yet another way—the real reason for the holiday has been distorted or forgotten. Both holidays have been perverted by those who don't even believe in God, but just want to have a good party! So let's try to set the record straight.

Chapter One

Hanukkah

Hanukkah is not a feast of the Lord. In fact, it's not even mentioned in the Tenach (the Old Testament). We are introduced to Hanukkah in John 10:22, when Jesus was in Jerusalem for "The Feast of Dedication."

Whatever its name, Hanukkah commemorates the rededication of the Second Temple after it had been defiled by the Seleucid dictator Antiochus Epiphanes in 163 BC. The story of the occupation of the Seleucids and their subsequent defeat is recorded in the Book of the Maccabees and Josephus' "History of the Jewish Wars." (See also the prophecies of Daniel chapters 9:27-12:13, which is so historically accurate that some believe Daniel could not have written it.)

Today the eight-day celebration of Hanukkah traditionally revolves around the lighting of candles to recall a miracle which *never* happened!

The legend says that when the Temple was ready to be rededicated, only a single day's supply of oil lasted for eight days, until a new supply of oil could be made.

Based on this legend, Hanukkah is often called "The Festival of Lights," when Jewish people light candles, increasing in number, for each of the eight days of the celebration.

Now while the legend of the oil might have happened, the truth is sooo much better. Indeed there was a miracle connected with Hanukkah—the miracle of God's protection, provision and power—in other words, the miracle of His love.

SO WHAT REALLY DID HAPPEN?

In the year 163 BC, Israel was ruled by the Greek tyrant, Antiochus Epiphanes. His hatred of the Jewish people, their religion and their God, knew no bounds. Eventually, as recorded by Daniel (9:27) and referred to by Jesus (Matthew 24:15), Antiochus defiled the Temple by erecting a statue of Zeus (which looked remarkably like himself) and demanding worship. The burnt altar was also desecrated by the sacrifice of swine.

Something had to be done. The encroachment of the Hellenistic culture had to be stopped. War was declared.

But in those days Israel did not have a mighty army. The IDF didn't exist. In fact, there was no army at all to fight against the mighty power of Greece. Nevertheless, there was a group of simple men and women (farmers, mothers, and merchants) who were ready to fight for God. They were determined to bring His righteousness and holiness back to the people, to Jerusalem and to the Temple. They fought bravely and persistently under the inspired leadership of Judas, nicknamed "Maccabee, The Hammer."

The battle continued for three years, until God gave them a supernatural victory.

Their first priority was to reclaim and cleanse their beloved Temple. Then the Temple needed to be rededicated to God.

Because the temples of Solomon and Zerubbabel were dedicated during the Feast of Booths (or in Hebrew, Sukkot), the people worked hard to finish the repairs so they could do the same.

They could not, so they did the next best thing; they adapted the traditions of Sukkot (The Festival of Booths), which had been celebrated just a few months before. In fact, originally Hanukkah was called "Sukkot of Chislev" (the Hebrew month of December).

So the truth about Hanukkah is that the eight days of celebration and the lighting of candles was not based on a miraculous supply of oil, but rather on the influence of Sukkot.

Sukkot was celebrated for eight days (Leviticus 23). Based on the prophecies in Ezekiel and Zechariah, lights illuminated the Temple and all of Jerusalem during Sukkot. Consequently, during the eight days of Hanukkah, the same lights were joyously lit!

So what was the miracle of Hanukkah? The victory of God's faithful triumph over evil. What is the real reason for celebrating Hanukkah? ***God's faithful love!***

Grandma's "two cents"
I firmly believe in the miracle of the oil as I also firmly believe in the Miracle of Messiah's birth. Without Hanukkah there would be no Christmas! ♥
Grandma

Chapter Two

The Hanukkah Christmas Connection

Actually, there is a historical connection between Hanukkah and Christmas. It was during the celebration of Hanukkah in the year 32 (about two hundred years later), that Yeshua announced most clearly that He was the long-awaited Messiah.

> *Then came the Feast of Dedication at Jerusalem. It was winter, and Jesus was in the temple area walking in Solomon's Colonnade. The Jews gathered around him, saying, "How long will you keep us in suspense? If you are the Messiah, tell us plainly."*

After their victory, Judas and his family (the Hasmoneans) ruled Israel. Soon they proved to be as corrupt as the Seleucids. Obviously Judas was not the promised Messiah, as many in Israel had hoped.

Sadly, many had forgotten that God had said HE would be their Savior, Redeemer, and Deliverer. Just has He had for Abraham and Isaac, He would provide the lamb. That Lamb would be a Shepherd/King like David. He would be a Deliverer/Prophet like Moses, a Priest like Melchizedek, the Glory of Israel and the Light to the Gentiles.

The coming of that Lamb is what Christmas is all about. I'd rather rename this holiday to better reflect its meaning...the "Celebration of the Incarnation.[1]" God becoming a man is the miracle of Christmas—God's love.

For God so loved the world that he gave his one and only Son, that whoever believes in him shall not perish but have eternal life

—John 3:16

Antiochus was, to put it nicely, CRAZY. He considered himself to be God. He named himself Epiphanes, meaning *god in the flesh.* But then, many today consider themselves to be "god" or at least "***a*** god."

But only God is God. Only His word established the heavens and the earth. It was He who created man out of the earth and breathed life into him. It is God who holds all things together, who establishes the boundary for the seas and for nations, and who raises up kings and destroys kingdoms. He says "Rain!" and it rains. The same for the snow, the hail, and the winds. He

1. The word "incarnation" means *the assumption of human form.* God became a man in contrast to the teaching of some that man can become a god.

knows every star...by name! It is God alone who can bind up broken hearts and fill them with hope, peace, and love.

God is love. His love is perfect; He is the very definition of love. While we cannot understand Him or all of His ways, He is good and brings good to those He loves and has called according to His purpose. There is nothing—no wicked, evil, horrible, hateful, painful experience that He cannot bring good out of.

Antiochus wasn't God; neither was he the Messiah. Moses wasn't God. While he did deliver the people from the bondage of Israel, he couldn't deliver them from the bondage of their sins. Judas Maccabee restored the Temple, but he couldn't restore the people's relationship with God.

These men were not Israel's Savior, nor were they God. Neither are the many who have proclaimed themselves to be God. Only God is God.

It was God in His love and mercy Who brought His people out of Egypt ***and*** out of the power and punishment of their sins. It was because of love that God gave Himself to Israel (and to the world[2]) to be their Savior, reconciling them to Himself , thus restoring broken hearts and broken lives.

It was out of love to Abraham, Isaac, and Jacob that God had promised David:

> *I will maintain my love to him (Israel) forever, and my covenant with him will never fail. I will establish his line forever, his throne as long as the heavens endure. If his sons forsake My law and do not follow My statutes, if they violate My decrees and fail to keep My commands,*

2. While God came to the world through the descendants of Abraham, Isaac, and Jacob, His love and provision of salvation applies EQUALLY to all mankind. Love does not discriminate, or consider one person above another. "*In Yeshua, there is neither man nor woman, Jew nor Gentile, slave nor free*" (Galatians 3:28)

I will punish their sin with the rod, their iniquity with flogging; but I will not take My love from him, nor will I ever betray My faithfulness. I will not violate My covenant or alter what My lips have uttered.

—Psalm 89:28-35

God made the same promises many times in Israel's history:

That He would be a Father to Israel and Israel would be His firstborn son

- That He would love them with an everlasting love
- That He would provide Himself as the atonement for their sins
- That He would be their Savior, being afflicted with all their afflictions
- That He would be their Redeemer, being the ransom for their sins
- That He would:
    - Bind up the brokenhearted,
    - Proclaim freedom for the captives & release from darkness the prisoners,
    - Comfort all who mourn,
    - Provide for those who grieve in Zion,
    - Bestow on them a crown of beauty instead of ashes,
    - The oil of gladness instead of mourning, and a garment of praise instead of a spirit of despair.

According to God's plan (Leviticus 17:11), there could be no forgiveness of sin and hence reconciliation to God without a sacrifice. Yet God had promised to BE the atonement. Here is the great mystery of all time...God became a man—***at the same time*** all God and all man—so that His blood would provide the atonement.

There are no logical explanations of what happened over 2,000 years ago in the Israeli town of Bethlehem. Faith is not based in the mind, but in the heart. Yet faith is not blind or stupid. There are enough evidences to believe that which we cannot understand. Faith is best expressed by the poet, the song writer, and the writers of the Holy Bible.

This is their story:

> *From the beginning was the Word. And the Word was with God. The Word was and is God. God and the Word from everlasting to everlasting.*

Separate but One. Different but the same. Understanding yet misunderstood. All knowing yet unknown. Manifested but mysterious. Hidden but seen. Giving but demanding. Loving, gracious, compassionate, righteous, holy, perfect, merciful, and just.

> *Everything was created by God and through the Word. Eternal life is in Him and this life gives light to all*[3] *people. His life is the light that shines through the darkness and the darkness can never extinguish it.*

> *He came to His own, but they didn't recognize Him or accept Him. Only a few would welcome and receive Him. But to all who did receive Him, He gave the right to become children of God. All they needed to do was to believe in (love, trust and obey) His name.*

---

3. See previous note.

All those who believe this are reborn—not a physical rebirth resulting from human passion or plan—but from the will of God.

And the Word became flesh and lived among us, full of loving forgiveness and truth. No one has actually seen God, but of course his only Son has, for He was face to face with God at the beginning. And now we have seen His glory…

Chapter Three

The Beginning of the Gospel about Yeshua

THE MESSIAH,

THE SON OF GOD,

THE ROOT OF JESSE,

THE ROD OF DAVID,

THE BRIGHT MORNING STAR,

THE ALPHA & OMEGA,

THE KING OF KINGS & LORD OF LORDS,

THE COMMANDER OF THE HOSTS,

THE GOOD SHEPHERD,

THE DOOR,

THE WAY & THE TRUTH & THE LIFE,

THE LIGHT OF THE WORLD,

LIVING WATERS, etc.

This is the record of the family of Yeshua Messiah, a descendant of King David, and of Abraham. There were fourteen generations in all from Abraham to David, fourteen from David to the exile to Babylon, and fourteen from the exile to the Messiah.

At the right time in history, God sent the angel Gabriel to Nazareth, a town in Galilee, to a virgin named Mary. Mary was engaged to be married to a man named Joseph, a descendant of King David.

Gabriel appeared to her and said,

> *"Greetings! Congratulations, you are greatly blessed. The Lord is with you."*

Mary was confused and disturbed by his words and tried to think what the angel could mean.

> *"Don't be frightened, Mary," the angel told her, "for God has decided to greatly bless you. Very soon now you will become pregnant and have a baby boy, and you are to name Him 'Yeshua.' He will be very great and will be called the Son of the Most High. The Lord God will give him the throne of his father David*

and He will reign over the house of Jacob forever. His Kingdom will never end."

[Several months earlier Gabriel had said to Mary's cousin Elizabeth that she too would have a son. Elizabeth (like Sarah) had been barren and was now in her old age. Like Isaac, this would be a very special child. God told the parents to name this child John. John's destiny to prepare the way for the Messiah had been foretold by the Hebrew prophets and, upon his birth, was affirmed by his father, Zechariah:

"Blessed be the Lord, the God of Israel; He has come to visit His people and has redeemed them. He is sending us a Mighty Savior from the royal line of His servant David, just as He promised through His holy prophets long ago, to save us from our enemies, from all who hate us.

He has been merciful to our ancestors, yes, to Abraham himself, by remembering His sacred promise to him, and by granting us the privilege of serving God fearlessly, freed from our enemies, and by making us holy and acceptable, ready to stand in His presence forever.

And you, my little son, shall be called the 'prophet of the glorious God', for you will prepare the way for the Messiah. You will tell His people how to find salvation through forgiveness of their sins. All this will be because the love of our God is very tender, and heaven's dawn is about to break upon us, to give light to those who sit in darkness and death's shadow, and to guide us to the path of peace."]

Mary asked the angel, "How will this be, since I am a virgin?"

The angel answered,

> *"The Holy Spirit will come upon you, and the power of the Most High will overshadow you. So the baby born shall be holy and will be called the Son of God. Even Elizabeth your relative is going to have a child in her old age, and she who was said to be barren is in her sixth month. For nothing is impossible with God."*

Mary answered, "I am the Lord's servant. I am willing to do whatever He wants. May everything you said come true." Then the angel left her.

Mary became pregnant. Even though she and Joseph were to be married, they had never come together!

Then Joseph, being a strict man, decided to break the engagement, but to do it quietly as he didn't want to publicly disgrace or embarrass Mary.

As he lay awake considering this, he fell into a dream and saw an angel standing beside him.

> *"Joseph, son of David," the angel said, "don't hesitate to take Mary as your wife. For the child within her has been conceived by the Holy Spirit. And she will have a Son and you shall name Him Yeshua (meaning God saves) because HE will save His people from their sins.*

This will fulfill God's message through His prophets [1]—

1. For a partial listing of the prophecies concerning Yeshua, see Appendix.

'The virgin shall give birth to a Son and He shall be called "Emmanuel" meaning God is with us.'

When Joseph woke up, he did what the angel of the Lord had commanded him and brought Mary home to be his wife, but she remained a virgin until her son was born.

And Mary said,

"Oh, how I praise the Lord. How I rejoice in God my Savior. For He saw me, His humble servant girl and now from one generation to another, people shall call me blessed of God.

For God, the Mighty Holy One, has done great things to me. His mercy goes on from generation to generation, to all who love and revere Him.

His mighty arm is so powerful. He scatters the proud and the arrogant ones. He has torn princes from their thrones and exalted the lowly. He has satisfied the hungry hearts and sent the rich away with empty hands.

He has helped His servant Israel. He has not forgotten His promise to be merciful. For He promised our fathers--Abraham and his children--to be merciful to them forever."

When Mary was in her final month, Caesar Augustus, the Roman Emperor, issued a decree that a census should be taken of the entire Roman world. And everyone went to his own town to register.

Because Joseph was a member of the royal line, he had to go to Bethlehem in Judea (King David's ancient home) journeying there from the Galilean village of Nazareth. He took Mary with him.

While they were there, the time came for the baby to be born, but there was no room for them in the inn. So when she gave birth to her firstborn, a son, she wrapped Him in cloths and placed Him in a manger.

That night some shepherds were in the field outside the village, guarding their flocks of sheep. Suddenly an angel appeared among them and the entire sky looked like it was on fire. Even the ground around them was shining with the glory of the Lord. They were very frightened, but the angel reassured them.

The angel said to them,

> *"Do not be afraid. I bring you good news. The greatest news—the most joyful news ever announced, and it's for everyone.*
>
> *The Savior—yes the Messiah—the Lord, has been born tonight in Bethlehem! How will you recognize Him? This will be a sign to you: you will find a baby wrapped in cloths and lying in a manger."*

Suddenly the angel was joined by a vast host of others—the armies of heaven. All of them were singing and praising God and saying:

"GLORY TO GOD IN THE HIGHEST, AND ON EARTH PEACE TO MEN WHO PLEASE HIM"

When the angels had left them and gone back into heaven, the shepherds said to one another, "Let's go to Bethlehem and see this thing that has happened, which the Lord has told us about."

They ran to the village and found their way to Mary and Joseph. And there was the baby, lying in the manger. The shepherds told everyone what had happened and what the angel had said to them about this child. All who heard the shepherds' story expressed astonishment, but Mary quietly treasured these things in her heart and often thought about them.

Then the shepherds went back again to their fields and flocks, praising God for the visit of the angels and because they had seen the child--just as the angel had told them.

Eight days later at the baby's circumcision ceremony, He was named Yeshua, the name given to Him by the angel before He was even conceived.

When the time came for Mary's purification offering at the Temple, as required by the Law of Moses after the birth of a child, His parents took Him to Jerusalem to present Him to the Lord. In these laws God had said, "If a woman's first child is a boy, he shall be dedicated to the Lord."

At that time, Yeshua's parents also offered their sacrifice for purification—"either a pair of turtledoves or two young pigeons", which was the legal requirement.

That day a man named Simeon, a Jerusalem resident, was in the Temple. He was a good man, very devout, filled with the Holy Spirit and constantly expecting the Messiah to come soon because the Holy Spirit had revealed to him that he would not die until he had seen him—God's anointed King.

That day, the Holy Spirit had impelled Simeon to go to the Temple, and so, when Mary and Joseph arrived to present the baby Jesus to the Lord in obedience to the Law, Simeon was there and took the child in his arms, praising God saying,

> *"Lord, now I can die content. For I have seen Him as You promised me I would. He is the Light that will shine upon the nations, and He will be the glory of Your people Israel!"*

Joseph and Mary just stood there, marveling at what was being said about Yeshua. Then Simeon blessed them and said to Mary, His mother:

> *"A sword shall pierce your soul, for this child shall be rejected by many in Israel, and that will be their undoing. But He will be the greatest joy of many others – both to Jews and Gentiles. And the deepest thoughts of many hearts shall be revealed."*

A prophetess, Anna, the daughter of Phanuel, of the tribe of Asher, was also there that day. She was very old;

she had lived with her husband seven years after her marriage, and then was a widow until she was eighty-four. She never left the Temple, but worshipped night and day, fasting and praying.

She came along just as Simeon was talking with Mary and Joseph, and she also began thanking God and telling everyone in Jerusalem, who had been waiting for the coming of the Savior. She told them, "The Messiah has come!"

When Joseph and Mary had done everything required by the Law of the Lord, they returned to Galilee to their own town of Nazareth. And Yeshua grew and became strong; He was filled with wisdom, and the grace of God was upon Him.

While Yeshua was still a baby, wise men from the east came to Jerusalem and asked, "Where is the One who has been born King of the Jews?" We saw His star in the east and have come to worship Him."

When Herod the king heard these things he was troubled, and Jerusalem was filled with rumors. Herod called a meeting of the religious leaders and asked them,

"Did the Hebrew prophets tell us where the Messiah would be born?"

"Yes, in Bethlehem," they said. "This is what the prophet Micah wrote."

> ***"You, Bethlehem, in the land of Judah, are by no means least among the rulers of Judah; but out of you will come a ruler who will be the Shepherd of My people Israel, and whose origins are from of old, from ancient times.***

He will be the Servant of the Lord to restore the tribes of Jacob and be a light for the Gentiles, that He might bring His salvation to the ends of the earth.

The zeal of the LORD Almighty will accomplish this!"

After the wise men had heard this, they went on their way,

and the star they had seen in the east went ahead of them until it stopped over the place where the child was. When they came to the house, they saw the child with His mother Mary and they bowed down and worshipped Him. Then they opened their treasures and presented Him with gifts of gold and of incense and of myrrh.

And since that day, millions of people, from Jerusalem to the outer regions of the world, both Jews and Gentiles have continued to worship Him.

For God has sworn in His holiness,

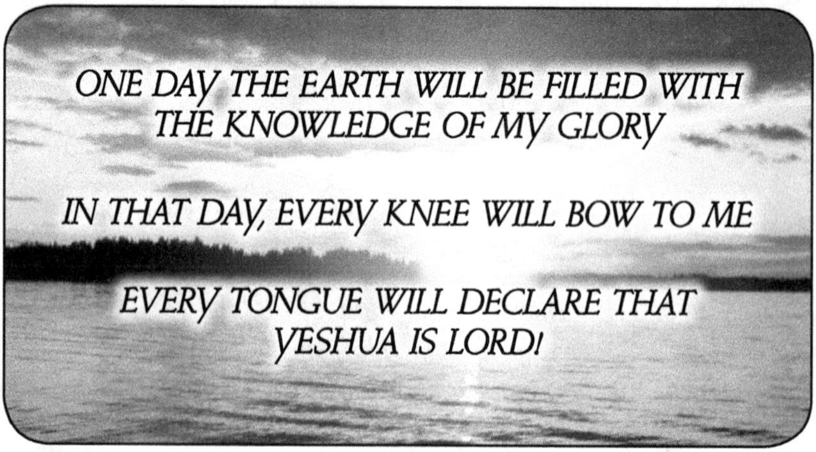
ONE DAY THE EARTH WILL BE FILLED WITH THE KNOWLEDGE OF MY GLORY
IN THAT DAY, EVERY KNEE WILL BOW TO ME
EVERY TONGUE WILL DECLARE THAT YESHUA IS LORD!

Chapter Four

The Incarnation

Most scholars agree that Yeshua was born somewhere around the time of the Feasts of the Lord in the fall. One way to reach this conclusion is through the story in Luke 1 concerning the birth of John the Baptist. From reading 1 Chronicles 24, it is possible to know when John the Baptist's father Zechariah, who belonged to the priestly division of Abijah, was serving in the Temple. We also know that six months later the angel Gabriel visited Mary (Miriam in Hebrew) and she became pregnant by the Holy Spirit. This information brings us to the seventh month on the Jewish calendar as the time of the incarnation of God.

We also have some amazing information from the constellation of the stars. First of all, the Magi (wise men) had seen the star of the King of the Jews in the East and had come to Jerusalem to look for Him. Secondly, the Book of Revelation, chapter 12, also speaks about a sign in the heavens connected with the birth of Messiah.

God created the stars, which includes the planets, to serve as signs.

> *"And God said, 'Let there be lights in the expanse of the sky to separate the day from the night, and let them serve as signs to mark seasons and days and years.'"*
>
> *—Genesis 1:4*

Psalm 19:1-4 says,

> *"The heavens declare the glory of God, the skies proclaim the work of His hands. Day after day they pour forth speech; night after night they display knowledge. There is no speech or language where their voice is not heard. Their voice goes out into all the earth, their words to the ends of the world."*

Before the Bible was written, God had already written the Gospel story in the stars. Respected Bible teachers such as Chuck Missler ("Signs in the Heavens") and Dr. D. James Kennedy ("The Real Meaning of the Zodiac"), point out that every civilization in history has always referred to the same constellations of the stars. The only reasonable explanation for this is that God taught Adam the meaning behind the stars, which was then handed down to succeeding generations.

The Gospel message is clearly seen in the Zodiac, beginning with the constellation of Virgo, the virgin, and ending with Leo, the King. This message was later perverted in Babylon into the reading of horoscopes to predict future events, which God strictly condemns as a demonic, occult practice.

The prophet Daniel was the chief of the magi in Babel. Most certainly he taught these magi the truths about the stars, which is the reason that some of them came to Jerusalem to search for the Messiah when He was born (Matthew 2:1-2).

Three Bible passages with Messianic prophecies give us the explanation about the star of "the one"—King of the Jews—the Messiah that the magi had seen.

- Numbers 24:17-19
- Genesis 49:8-10
- Psalm 110:1-4

We see in Numbers 24, that a star, also called a scepter, will come out from Jacob. In Genesis 49 we see that this scepter narrows down to coming from the tribe of Judah, who is called a lion, and, in Psalm 110, we see that the Messiah will come after the order of Melchizedek, meaning "King of Righteousness."

Jupiter, called Zedek in Hebrew and meaning 'righteous,' has always been connected with the Messiah, the "Righteous One." The brightest star in Leo, the Lion, which is a symbol for Judah, is Regiel, which means "king" (in Hebrew *Melech*).

The Magi said, "*We saw his star in the east.*" On September 12, on the Feast of Trumpets, in the year 3 BC, Regiel (Melech) and Jupiter (Zedek), began to make a helical rising together as one star, forming Melchizedek appearing between the feet of Leo (Judah), on the eastern horizon just before sunrise. This helical rising of Regiel and Jupiter happens once in about 80 years. However, within one year it happened two more times, in connection with the Feasts of Purim and Shavuot (Pentecost).

But something else also happened in the heavens that night of the Feast of Trumpets, 3 BC. Between 6:18 and 7:39 local Jerusalem time, in the evening of September 11, just as the Feast began, Virgo was "clothed in the sun" with the new moon under her feet, exactly as described in Revelation 12:1-5.

That year the sun was in the sign of Virgo for twenty days, between August 27 and September 15, but for only about one and a half hours during that time was the moon under the feet of Virgo. It happened exactly when the Feast of Trumpets began. This was most likely the exact time that Mary was in labor according to Revelation 12, giving birth to the Messiah while the watchmen on the walls of Jerusalem announced the new moon, and the shofars were blowing! Little did they know what had just taken place a couple of miles away!

According to Jewish tradition, Adam, who is also called the son of God in Scripture (Luke 3:38), was created by God on the Feast of Trumpets. How fitting that the last Adam was also born on the same day! And just as Yeshua one day will return as King with the trumpet call of God, He also came the first time at the sound of the trumpet. The arrival of a king was usually announced with trumpets.

It is amazing how exactly in detail God fulfills His word!

There is even more to be learned from the stars. In the story of the Magi, Matthew says that the star "*stopped over the place where the child was.*" (Matthew 2:9) After the third joint appearance in one year of Melech and Zedek as one star on May 8, (Pentecost) in 2 BC, Jupiter (Zedek) began to move west in the sky in the latter part of June. It is very likely that the Magi decided to follow the star until they arrived in Jerusalem, a journey which took Ezra about four months. Probably the Magi arrived in Jerusalem in early winter.

Herod secretly asked the Magi about the exact time that the star had appeared. Later, in his effort to murder the newborn King, he ordered that every boy in the vicinity of Bethlehem "*two years old and under*" should be put to death "*in accordance with the time he had learned from the Magi*" (Matthew 2:16). On December 25, 2 BC, Jupiter stopped in its westward course in the sky. From the viewpoint in Jerusalem, it appeared to stop over Bethlehem, "*The place where the child was*" (verse 9).

At the time of the magi's visit, Jesus was not a baby anymore, as He had been born more than a year earlier. He was a boy of fifteen months.

Here is even more information declaring the wonders of our God. If Yeshua was born on September 11, 3 BC, He would have been conceived by the Holy Spirit 38 weeks earlier, around December 19, 4 BC right in the midst of Chanukah at the time of the new moon. The Light of the World became flesh during Chanukah, the holiday of dedication when Jerusalem is illuminated by lights. How appropriate that the Light of the world was formed by the Holy Spirit in Mary's womb during this holiday!

Yeshua was born as a man and died as a man, but His conception and His resurrection are the proofs that He is the Messiah, the Son of God.

> *"The angel answered, 'The Holy Spirit will come upon you, and the power of the Most High will overshadow you; so the holy one to be born will be called the Son of God.'" (Luke 1:35)... who as to his human nature was a descendant of David, and who through the Spirit of holiness was declared with power to be the Son of God by His resurrection from the dead: Jesus Christ our Lord."*
>
> *—Romans 1:4*

The Celebration of Incarnation is very important. It should not come as a surprise that the enemy wants to distract people either through pagan rituals, theological disagreements, cultural traditions and conflicts, and a frenzy of commercialism—anything to distort the real message and miracle.

It is also a feast of great prophetic significance. Galatians 4:4 says, "*But when the time had fully come, God sent his Son, born of a woman, born under law to redeem those under law...*"

Whether we celebrate on December 25th or during the Feast of Sukkot, the fact remains...

- God became a man
- The Creator became created
- The King became a Servant
- The Holy entered the realm of the common

[Yeshua] "Who, being in very nature God, did not consider equality with God something to be [stolen], made himself nothing, taking the very nature of a servant, being made in human likeness. And being found in appearance as a man, he humbled himself and became obedient to death--even death on a cross!.... that we might receive the full rights of sons"... God demonstrates his own love for us in this: While we were still sinners, Messiah died for us...God has poured out his love into our hearts by the Holy Spirit, whom he has given us...

Chapter Four

Jesus and Hanukkah

Among the many misconceptions Jewish people have today about Jesus (or in Hebrew, Yeshua) one is that He never claimed to be God.

That's simply not true. Jesus did claim to be God. He repeated that claim often and in various ways. It was during the holiday of Hanukkah, as recorded in John's gospel (10:22-39) that Jesus gave the final and most clear declaration of His deity.

So why are these claims ignored? Because people don't want to be confronted or confused with FACTS—they've already made their minds.

Often facts are not used in the quest for truth. Especially in the arena of the spiritual; we rely on our feelings, values, fears, and/or traditions to lead us. We deny the absoluteness of truth and make it personal and relative.

But truth must align itself to factual reality, bounded by time and space—regardless of how it feels, or what demands it makes upon our lives.

The truth is that Jesus was heard and understood. There were those who didn't like what He said and tried to either stone Him or seize Him. Others knew He was telling the truth and believed. Confronted and challenged each person had to make a choice. The same is still true today. Each of us has to make a choice about Jesus.

It may not be a coincidence that at the core of the words "hear" and "heart" is the word ear. What goes through the ear seems to be processed by the heart.

THE CONTEXT OF JESUS' CLAIMS OF DEITY

> *Then came the Feast of Dedication at Jerusalem. It was winter, and Jesus was in the temple area walking in Solomon's Colonnade.* —John 10:22-23

During the Feast of Dedication (Hanukkah) that year Messianic expectations were almost palpable. Almost two hundred years had passed since the first Hanukkah celebration. Not much had changed. The Jews were still under foreign domination. There were still great conflicts within the Jewish community itself. They were desperate for their promised Messiah. As they had through Moses and later Judas Maccabee, they sought political emancipation so that they would enjoy spiritual freedom

Beyond their need for the Messiah, many knew the prophecy of Daniel (Daniel 9:25-26a). Simple arithmetic argued that *this* would be the year that the Messiah would be "*cut off, but not for Himself.*" Israel's faithful had been watching and waiting (Luke 2:25, 36). They (like Bethlehem's shepherds and some Gentile wise men) claimed they had found Him thirty years before this winter day (Luke 2:8; Matthew 2:11).

The Jews gathered around him, saying, "How long will you keep us in suspense? If you are the Christ, [Messiah] tell us plainly."
—John 10:24

The people said they were in suspense. Yet during the previous three months, since the Feast of Tabernacles (Sukkot) Jesus had been making very strong claims of deity. For those with a heart and ears to hear, the Messianic implications could not be ignored.

Thus the question put before Him on this day was revealing. It betrayed their refusal to accept the facts. Therefore Jesus could answer them:

Jesus answered, "I did tell you, but you do not believe."
—John 10:25

Antiochus had claimed to be god in the flesh, but then couldn't back up those claims with proof. Jesus who WAS God in the flesh easily proved His deity through His words, His works and His witness.

THE CLAIMS OF JESUS OF BEING GOD, THE MESSIAH

Although many Jews are still looking for a human deliverer, God had said through His prophets that He would be the Messiah.

You will drink the milk of nations and be nursed at royal breasts. Then you will know that I, the LORD, am your Savior, your Redeemer, the Mighty One of Jacob.
—Isaiah 60:16

But God will redeem my life from the grave; He will surely take me to Himself.
—Psalm 49:15

By applying the words and works of God to Himself, Jesus claimed to be the Messiah.

JESUS' WORDS

- He said that He was the source of the Spirit and of living water:

  On the last and greatest day of the Feast, Jesus stood and said in a loud voice, "If anyone is thirsty, let him come to Me and drink. Whoever believes in Me, as the Scripture has said, streams of living water will flow from within him." —John 7:37-38

  Thousands of years before, through the prophets God had said that He was the source of living water. From, in, and through Him would come the Spirit and the river of life.

  *Surely God is my **salvation;** I will trust and not be afraid. The LORD, the LORD, is my strength and my song; he has become my **salvation.**" With joy you will draw water from the wells of **salvation.***
  —Isaiah 12:2 (emphasis added)

  For with You is the fountain of life; in Your light we see light. —Psalm 36:9

  My people have committed two sins: They have forsaken Me, the spring of living water, and have dug their own cisterns, broken cisterns that cannot hold water.
  —Jeremiah 2:13

O LORD, the hope of Israel, all who forsake You will be put to shame. Those who turn away from You will be written in the dust because they have forsaken the LORD, the spring of living water. —Jeremiah 17:13

For I will pour water on the thirsty land, and streams on the dry ground; I will pour out my Spirit on your offspring, and My blessing on your descendants. —Isaiah 44:3

He said that He was the Light of the world

When Jesus spoke again to the people, He said, "I am the light of the world. Whoever follows Me will never walk in darkness, but will have the light of life." —John 8:12

He who created light and separated it from the darkness was Himself light. John the Baptizer was merely echoing the words of the prophets before Him when he said about Jesus, "In Him was life, and the life was the light of men."

The sun will no more be your light by day, nor will the brightness of the moon shine on you, for the LORD will be your everlasting light, and your God will be your glory. Your sun will never set again, and your moon will wane no more; the LORD will be your everlasting light, and your days of sorrow will end. —Isaiah 60:19-20

The Light of Israel will become a fire, their Holy One a flame; in a single day it will burn and consume his thorns and his briers. —Isaiah 10:17

Do not gloat over me, my enemy! Though I have fallen, I will rise. Though I sit in darkness, the LORD will be my light. —*Micah 7:8*

Because I have sinned against him, I will bear the LORD's wrath, until He pleads my case and establishes my right. He will bring me out into the light; I will see his righteousness. —*Micah 7:10*

... the people living in darkness have seen a great light; on those living in the land of the shadow of death a light has dawned. —*Isaiah 9:1-2; Matthew 4:16*

- He said that He was the Good Shepherd

I am the good shepherd. The good shepherd lays down his life for the sheep. —*John 10:11*

The prophet Ezekiel (chapter 34) had compared the bad shepherds leading Israel with God, the Good Shepherd of Israel. Even today many people know and love Psalm 23 which defines the Lord God as The Shepherd. Jesus was taking that title upon Himself.

The LORD is my shepherd, I shall not be in want. —*Psalm 23:1*

God who has been my shepherd all my life to this day... —*Genesis 48:14*

... the Mighty One of Jacob, the Shepherd, the Rock of Israel... *Genesis 49:24*

Hear us, O Shepherd of Israel, you who lead Joseph like a flock; you who sit enthroned between the cherubim, shine forth. —*Psalm 80:1*

Furthermore, as Ezekiel recorded God's ownership over His sheep, Jesus was exercising the same ownership:

Jesus answered, " ...but you do not believe because you are not My sheep. My sheep listen to My voice; I know them, and they follow Me. —*John 10:25-27*

For this is what the Sovereign LORD says: "I myself will search for My sheep and look after them. As a shepherd looks after his scattered flock when he is with them, so will I look after My sheep. I will shepherd the flock with justice." —*Ezekiel 34:11-16*

JESUS' WORKS

Jesus reiterated that both His words and His works testified that He was Messiah.

Jesus answered, "I did tell you, but you do not believe. The miracles I do in my Father's name speak for me.
—*John 10:25*

- He exercised power over creation
  - He turned water into wine (John 2:1-11)
  - He calmed a storm by speaking to it (Mark 4:35-41)

- He walked on water (Matthew 14:22-33)
- He fed thousands with a few fish and loaves of bread (Matt 14:15-21 &15:32-39)
- He raised the dead (John 11:1-54)
- Lazarus had been dead for days (John 11:1-54)
- Raises a widow's son as he was being carried for burial (Luke 7:11-16)
- He healed the lame, the dumb, the blind
  - Matt 9:27-33
  - Matt 14:14
  - Matt 15: 30
  - Luke 13:10-17
  - Mark 7:31-37
- He set the captives free
  - Demoniac in the synagogue (Mark 1:23-26)
  - Demoniacs in Gadara (Matt 8:28-34)
- He forgave sins
  - *She will give birth to a son, and you are to give him the name Jesus, because He will save his people from their sins* (Matthew 1:21).
  - *When Jesus saw their faith, he said to the paralytic, "Son, your sins are forgiven. "Now some teachers of the law were sitting there, thinking to themselves, "Why does this fellow talk like that? He's blaspheming! Who can forgive sins but God alone?"* (Mark 2:5-7)

✦ He had power over death:

- *And this is the will of Him who sent Me, that I shall lose none of all that He has given Me, but raise them up at the last day. For my Father's will is that everyone who looks to the Son and believes in Him shall have eternal life, and I will raise him up at the last day"* (John 6:39-40).
- *Jesus said to her, "I am the resurrection and the life. He who believes in Me will live, even though he dies; and whoever lives and believes in Me will never die"* (John 11:25-26).
- *I am the Living One; I was dead, and behold I am alive for ever and ever! And I hold the keys of death and Hades* (Revelation 1:18).

HIS SELF WITNESS

I and the Father are one. —John 10:30

It's clear from the record that Jesus was heard and understood.

> *Again the Jews picked up stones to stone him, but Jesus said to them, "I have shown you many great miracles from the Father. For which of these do you stone Me?"*
>
> *"We are not stoning you for any of these," replied the Jews, "but for blasphemy, because you, a mere man, claim to be God."* —John 10:31-33

They had heard. They just didn't like nor accept what they heard. So the problem was not obscurity but obstinacy. Jesus was being clear in His proclamation. He had been telling them that

He was their Messiah in every way possible for the last three years. He hadn't spoken in secret but to crowds of thousands.

In this His last public appearance for several months; Jesus was confronting the people with the hardness of their hearts. Their ears had heard but their hearts had refused to listen. It wasn't a hearing problem, it was a heart issue.

> *Jesus answered, "I did tell you, but you do not believe."*
> *—John 10:25*

> *To whom can I speak and give warning? Who will listen to me? Their ears are closed so they cannot hear. The word of the LORD is offensive to them; they find no pleasure in it.*
> *—Jeremiah 6:10*

The problem was the people's refusal to accept Him. Had they done so, their lives would have had to change. Jesus never gave the option of believing but not following Him. As God the Father, God the Son was demanding passionate love, total commitment, and complete dedication.

> *Hear, O Israel: The LORD our God, the LORD is one. Love the LORD your God with all your heart and with all your soul and with all your strength.*
> *—Deuteronomy 6:4-5*

> *If you love me, you will obey what I command.*
> *—John 14:15*

> *Anyone who loves his father or mother more than Me is not worthy of Me; anyone who loves his son or daughter more than Me is not worthy of Me; and anyone who does not take his cross and follow Me is not worthy of Me.*
> *—Matthew 10:37-38*

Then Jesus said to his disciples, "If anyone would come after Me, he must deny himself and take up his cross and follow Me. For whoever wants to save his life will lose it, but whoever loses his life for Me will find it."
—Matthew 16:24-25

Much was at stake. The people were being confronted with the truth about Jesus, about God, and about themselves. The Jewish people had been chosen by God to be His witnesses, to be holy unto Him. Hanukkah is a memorial to God's faithfulness to a remnant that chose, against persecution and torture, to stand firm in faith and be faithful to Him.

Hanukkah challenges us to make life choices. Moses, Joshua, and King David had challenged the people of their day to make a choice—life for death, God or the gods of the world. Was it with sadness or anger or resignation that Jesus confronted them with the result of their choice?

Jesus answered..."you are not My sheep. My sheep listen to My voice; I know them, and they follow Me."
—John 10:25-27

Their choice had eternal consequences. They had been looking for a political savior, but before them was the Savior of their souls. They had hardened their hearts to the ultimate promise of freedom and security:

I give them eternal life, and they shall never perish; no one can snatch them out of My hand. My Father, who has given them to Me, is greater than all; no one can snatch them out of my Father's hand. *—John 10:28-29*

Jesus continued pleading with them to make the right choice-the choice of faith:

Jesus answered them, "Is it not written in your Law, 'I have said you are gods?' If he called them 'gods,' to whom the word of God came—and the Scripture cannot be broken—what about the one whom the Father set apart as his very own and sent into the world? Why then do you accuse Me of blasphemy because I said, 'I am God's Son?' Do not believe Me unless I do what my Father does. But if I do it, even though you do not believe Me, believe the miracles that you may know and understand that the Father is in Me, and I in the Father."

—John 10:3-38

The Biblical account of Hanukkah, the holiday of Dedication, ends with another the miracle, the miracle of faith:

Then Jesus went back across the Jordan to the place where John had been baptizing in the early days. Here he stayed and many people came to Him. They said, "Though John never performed a miraculous sign, all that John said about this man was true." And in that place many believed in Jesus. *—John 10:40-42*

TWO QUESTIONS

So dear reader, Hanukkah presents two questions.

The first question is this, "**What will you do about Jesus?**" Jesus claimed to be the Messiah. He claimed He was God in the flesh. C.S. Lewis once wrote that we only have three choices about Jesus. He was a liar, a lunatic, or actually the Lord.

If Jesus was not speaking truth, He is the worst and most diabolical liar in history. Over the centuries, millions of people have willingly faced torture or a martyr's death because of their faith in Him.

If Jesus was not speaking truth He was a not simply a liar, He was a lunatic and did not, nor does not deserve the honor He has received.

Finally, if Jesus was speaking the truth, He ***is*** Lord. Which brings us to the second question, "**Will you follow Him?**" Hanukkah challenges us to be faithful to Jesus regardless of circumstances or consequences. Jesus expects and demands us to be holy and wholly dedicated to Him.

Jesus said, "*My sheep listen to My voice; I know them, and they follow Me.*" So are you hearing His voice and are you following Him? The prophet Daniel said, "Those who know their God will do mighty exploits."

Today we are facing challenging times, but not more challenging than the faithful Jewish remnant of 165 BC. They would not bow down to the pressures or persecutions of their society. Will you?

Jesus promises to be with us all times, with necessary grace and strength to accomplish His will. His love is sufficient.

During this holiday season, may you experience the miracle of God's love in and through Christ Jesus.

joanie

Appendix

PARTIAL LIST OF PROPHECIES CONCERNING YESHUA

The following is a partial list that was taken from the website: www.messiahrevealed.org

The Messiah would be the creator of all.	Psalm 102:25-27b	John 1:3
The Messiah would be Lord.	Psalm 110:1a	Matthew 22:41-45
The Messiah would be holy.	Daniel 9:24b	Luke 1:35
The Messiah would be God.	Psalm 45:6-7b Isaiah 7:14c Isaiah 40:3c Jeremiah 23:5-6b	Hebrews 1:8-9 John 12:45 John 10:30 John 13:13
The Messiah would be both God and man.	Jeremiah 23:5-6c	1 Timothy 3:16
The Messiah would be both God and man (the "Mighty God).	Isaiah 9:6d	John 10:30
The Messiah would be God.	Zechariah 11:10-11b; 12-13d	John 14:7; 12:45
The Messiah would be both God and man.	Zechariah 12:10b	John 10:30
The Messiah would be both God and man.	Zechariah 13:7c	John 14:9

God would have a Son.	Proverbs 30:4b	Matthew 3:16-17
The Messiah would be the Son of God.	Psalm 2:7a Psalm 2:12a	Luke 1:31-35 Matthew 17:5
The Messiah would be the Son of God.	2 Samuel 7:13-14	Matthew 3:16-17
The Messiah would be the Son of God.	1 Chronicles 17:13-14	John 12:28-30
The Messiah would be the Son of God.	Isaiah 9:6b	Luke 1:35
The Messiah would call God his Father.	Psalm 89:26	Matthew 11:27
The Messiah would be announced to his people 483 years, to the exact day, after the decree to rebuild the city of Jerusalem.	Daniel 9:25	John 12:12-13
The Messiah would be killed before the destruction of the temple.	Daniel 9:26c	Matthew 27:50-51
The Messiah would be born of the "seed" of a woman.	Genesis 3:15a	Luke 1:34-35
The Messiah would be born of a virgin.	Isaiah 7:14a	Luke 1:34-35
The Messiah would be born of a virgin.	Jeremiah 31:22	Matthew 1:18-20
The Messiah would be Immanuel, "God with us."	Isaiah 7:14b	Matthew 1:21-23
The Messiah would be called by his name before he was born.	Isaiah 49:1c	Luke 1:30-31

The Messiah would be a prophet.	Deuteronomy 18:15-19a	John 6:14
The Messiah would be a Priest in the order of Melchisedec.	Psalm 110:4	Hebrews 6:17-20
The Messiah would be Priest and King.	Zechariah 6:12-13	Hebrews 8:1
The Messiah would be a King.	Genesis 49:10b Numbers 24:17	John 1:49 John 19:19
The Messiah would be the messenger of the new covenant.	Malachi 3:1c	Luke 4:43
The Messiah would be the new covenant.	Isaiah 42:6c Jeremiah 31:31	Matthew 26:28 Matthew 26:28
The Messiah would come to make an end to sins.	Daniel 9:24a	Galatians 1:3-5
The Messiah would provide freedom from the bondage of sin and death.	Isaiah 61:1-2c	John 8:31-32
The Messiah would proclaim a period of grace.	Isaiah 61:1-2d	John 5:24
The Messiah would die for the sins of the world.	Isaiah 53:8d	1 John 2:2
The Messiah would die for the sins of the world.	Daniel 9:26b	Hebrews 2:9
The Messiah would give up his life to save mankind.	Isaiah 53:12b	Luke 23:46
The Messiah would be as a sacrificial lamb.	Isaiah 53:7c	John 1:29
The Messiah would be an offering for sin.	Isaiah 53:10b	Matthew 20:28

The Messiah's offering of himself would replace all sacrifices.	Psalm 40:6-8a	Hebrews 10:10-13
The Messiah's blood would be shed to make atonement for all.	Isaiah 52:15	Revelation 1:5
The Messiah would be the sin-bearer for all mankind.	Isaiah 53:6a	Galatians 1:4
The Messiah would be the sin-bearer for all mankind.	Isaiah 53:11d	Hebrews 9:28
The Messiah would be the sin-bearer for all mankind.	Isaiah 53:12d	2 Corinthians 5:21
The Messiah would bear and carry upon himself the sins of the world.	Isaiah 53:4b	1 Peter 2:24
The Messiah would bear the penalty for mankind's transgressions.	Isaiah 53:5a	Luke 23:33
The Messiah's sacrifice would provide peace between man and God.	Isaiah 53:5b	Colossians 1:20
The Messiah would justify man before God.	Isaiah 53:11c	Romans 5:8-9
The Messiah would be the intercessor between man and God.	Isaiah 59:15-16b	Matthew 10:32-33
The Messiah would intercede to God on behalf of mankind.	Isaiah 53:12e	Luke 23:34

The Messiah's atonement would enable believers to be his brethren.	Psalm 22:22	Hebrews 2:10-12
The Messiah would come to provide salvation.	Isaiah 59:15-16a	John 6:40
The Messiah would bring salvation.	Zechariah 9:9d	Luke 19:10
The Messiah would have a ministry to the "poor," the believing remnant.	Zechariah 11:7	Matthew 9:35-36
The Messiah would offer salvation to all mankind.	Joel 2:32	Romans 10:12-13
The Messiah would come to bring Israel back to God.	Isaiah 49:5b	Matthew 15:24
The Messiah would come to Zion as their Redeemer.	Isaiah 59:20	Luke 2:38
Those who refused to listen to the Messiah would be judged.	Deuteronomy 18:15-19c	John 12:48-50
The Messiah would reject those who did not believe in him.	Psalm 2:12b	John 3:36
The Messiah would be sacrificed upon the same mountain where God tested Abraham.	Genesis 22:14	Luke 23:33
The Messiah would be grouped with criminals.	Isaiah 53:12c	Luke 23:32
The Messiah's hands and feet would be pierced.	Psalm 22:16c	Matthew 27:38

The Messiah would pray for his enemies.	Psalm 109:4	Luke 23:34
The Messiah would be offered gall and vinegar.	Psalm 69:21a	Matthew 27:34
The Messiah's garments would be divided.	Psalm 22:18a	John 19:23-24
Lots would be cast for the Messiah's clothes.	Psalm 22:18b	John 19:23-24
The Messiah would be surrounded by Gentiles at his crucifixion.	Psalm 22:16a	Luke 23:36
The Messiah would be surrounded by Gentiles at his crucifixion.	Psalm 22:16b	Matthew 27:41-43
People would stare at the Messiah during crucifixion.	Psalm 22:17b	Luke 23:35
The Messiah would be thought to be cursed by God.	Isaiah 53:4c	Matthew 27:41-43
The Messiah would be mocked by people shaking their heads.	Psalm 22:7	Matthew 27:39
The Messiah would be mocked by people shaking their heads.	Psalm 109:25	Mark 15:29-30
Mockers would say of the Messiah, "he trusted God, let Him deliver him."	Psalm 22:8	Matthew 27:41-43
The Messiah would be crucified.	Psalm 22:14b	Matthew 27:35
The Messiah would cry out to God.	Psalm 22:1a	Matthew 27:46

The Messiah would be forsaken by God.	Psalm 22:1b	Mark 15:34
The Messiah would be surrounded by evil spirits.	Psalm 22:12-13	Colossians 2:15
The Messiah would thirst.	Psalm 22:15a Psalm 69:21b Psalm 22:15b	John 19:28 John 19:30
The Messiah would be killed.	Isaiah 53:8c Daniel 9:26a	Matthew 27:35
The Messiah would die a violent death.	Zechariah 13:7b	Matthew 27:35
None of the Messiah's bones would be broken.	Psalm 22:17a Psalm 34:20	John 19:32-33
The Messiah's body would be pierced.	Zechariah 12:10a	John 19:34-37
The Messiah's heart would be broken.	Psalm 69:20a	John 19:34
The Messiah's heart would burst, flowing with blood & water.	Psalm 22:14a	John 19:34
The Messiah would be buried in a rich man's grave.	Isaiah 53:9a	Matthew 27:57
The Messiah's body would not be subject to decay.	Psalm 16:8-10b	Acts 13:35-37
The Messiah would be resurrected.	Psalm 16:8-10a	Matthew 28:6
The Messiah would be resurrected and live forever.	Isaiah 53:10c	Mark 16:16

The Messiah would be resurrected by God.	Isaiah 55:3	Acts 13:34
Others would rise to life at the resurrection of the Messiah.	Isaiah 26:19	Matthew 27:52-53
The Messiah would be God's "firstborn."	Psalm 89:27	Mark 16:6
The Messiah would defeat death.	Isaiah 25:8 Hosea 13:14	Revelation 1:18 1 Corinthians 15:55-57
The Messiah would defeat Satan.	Genesis 3:15b	1 John 3:8
The Messiah would be justified by his righteousness.	Isaiah 50:8	1 Timothy 3:16
The Messiah would ascend into heaven.	Psalm 68:18a	Luke 24:51
The Messiah would ascend into heaven.	Daniel 7:13-14a	Acts 1:9-11
The Messiah would ascend and descend from heaven.	Proverbs 30:4a	John 3:13
The Messiah would be exalted to the presence of God.	Psalm 16:11	Acts 2:25-33
The Messiah would be resurrected and crowned as King.	Psalm 2:7c	Acts 13:30-33
The Messiah would be exalted by God with power and strength.	1 Samuel 2:10	Matthew 28:18
The Messiah would be at the right hand of God.	Psalm 80:17 Psalm 110:1b Psalm 110:5	Acts 5:31 Mark 16:19 1 Peter 3:21-22
The Messiah's throne would be everlasting.	1 Chronicles 17:11-12b	Luke 1:31-33
The Messiah's throne would be everlasting.	Psalm 45:6-7a Daniel 7:13-14c	Luke 1:31-33

Because of his sacrifice, the Messiah would be greatly exalted by God.	Isaiah 53:12a	Matthew 28:18
The Messiah would be highly exalted.	Isaiah 52:13b	Philippians 2:9-11
The Messiah would be highly exalted.	Daniel 7:13-14b	Ephesians 1:20-22
The Messiah would prosper.	Isaiah 53:10d	John 17:1-5
The Messiah would receive authority over all.	Psalm 2:8b	Matthew 28:18
The Messiah would be given authority over all things.	Psalm 8:6	Matthew 28:18
A vision of the Messiah in a glorified state.	Daniel 10:5-6	Revelation 1:13-16